PACEMAKER®

Practical English

WORKBOOK

Globe
Fearon

Upper Saddle River, New Jersey
www.globefearon.com

REVIEWERS

We thank the following educators, who provided valuable comments and suggestions during the development of this book:

Pacemaker Curriculum Advisor: Stephen Larsen, formerly of the University of Texas at Austin

Subject Area Consultants: M.B. Clarke, University of California, Davis, and A.G. Clarke, American River College, Sacramento

Executive Editor: Eleanor Ripp
Project Editor: Brian Hawkes
Assistant Editor: Alisa Brightman
Lead Designer: Tricia Battipede
Research Manager: Angela Darchi
Marketing Manager: Katie Erezuma
Production Editor: Angela Dion
Manufacturing Supervisor: Mark Cirillo
Cover Design: Tricia Battipede

About the Cover: English skills help people communicate effectively with one another. The images on the cover show the variety of ways that English skills are used in everyday life. Computers are used to give and receive information. "Help Wanted" ads show listings of available jobs. Daily planners help people organize themselves. Letters and postcards are mailed to keep in touch with loved ones. Job applications need to be filled in to get jobs. What are some other ways you use English skills in your life?

Pacemaker® Practical English, Third Edition

ISBN: 0-130-23600-4

Printed in the United States of America
2 3 4 5 6 7 8 9 10   05 04 03 02 01

GLOBE FEARON EDUCATIONAL PUBLISHER
Upper Saddle River, New Jersey
www.globefearon.com

Contents

A Note to the Student

Use this Workbook along with your *Pacemaker® Practical English* textbook. The exercises in this Workbook are linked to the skills in your textbook. This Workbook will help you do two things—practice and think critically. At the top of each exercise page, you will see that the exercise is labeled as either "Practice" or "Critical Thinking."

The "Practice" activities give you the opportunity to practice the skills you learned in your textbook. These activities will be similar to many of the activities in your textbook. The more you practice, the more you will remember.

The "Critical Thinking" activities will challenge you to think beyond what you learned in your textbook. Critical thinking—or, to put it another way, thinking critically—means putting information to use.

Your Workbook is a wonderful source of knowledge. By completing the activities, you will learn a great deal about practical English skills. The real value of this information will come when you have mastered these skills and put critical thinking to use.

Name _____ Date _____

1 ▶ Writing a Report

Skill 1.1

Exercise 1

Practice

The notes in the box are based on an article about Juliette Gordon Low, the founder of the Girl Scouts. Read the notes. Then use them to write a few paragraphs about Juliette Gordon Low.

> Juliette Gordon Low: Born 1860, in Savannah, Georgia. Nicknamed Daisy by an uncle. Had three sisters and two brothers. Father in cotton business. Mother was a homemaker. Lost hearing in one ear at age 25. A year later she married William Low. At wedding, guests threw rice. Grain landed in her good ear. Injury led to deafness. Became a widow. Married founder of the Boy Scouts, Lord Robert Baden-Powell. Founded the Girl Scouts in Savannah, Georgia, in 1912. Believed that camping and outdoor life were important in Girl Scouting. Girl Scouts played games, took nature hikes, went bird watching, learned first aid, went camping, learned to sew, and helped others. Died in 1927.

_____

_____

_____

_____

_____

_____

_____

_____

_____

_____

_____

_____

_____

1 ▶ Taking Notes on an Article
Skill 1.1

Exercise 2

Critical Thinking

A. Read the following article. Then take notes on it by writing answers to the questions listed below. Write important information only.

> Henry Ossawa Tanner knew he was doing the right thing when he left Philadelphia to go to Paris in January 1891. He was an excellent artist, and he felt that he would have a better chance of success in Paris. By the time he was 32, Tanner had already sold much of his own original art and was considered by many to be quite talented. However, Tanner knew it would be difficult to be successful in America.
>
> At the time, prejudice against African Americans was a source of great pain to Tanner. Although his background was more English than African, Tanner believed that his African side was the source of all his talents.
>
> Born in 1859, Tanner lived in Paris from 1891 until his death there in 1937. Today he is known mainly for his beautiful paintings based on themes from the Bible and on the ordinary lives of simple people. Some of his more famous paintings include *The Annunciation* and *The Banjo Lesson*. Among his portraits, the most famous ones are *Portrait of the Artist's Mother* and *Portrait of Booker T. Washington*. Each one shows Tanner's experiments with the use of light, which can be seen in many more of his paintings as well. Tanner was the first African American artist to become famous around the world.

Who? _____

What? _____

Why? _____

Where? _____

When? _____

How? _____

B. Think about the article. Write a good title for it.

_____

_____

1 ▶ Organizing Directions

Skill 1.2

Exercise 3

Practice

The directions for the recipe below are not in the correct order. Rewrite each set of directions in step-by-step order.

Scrambled Eggs
- First crack open two raw eggs and drop contents into a bowl.
- Heat some butter or oil in a pan before adding the eggs.
- When eggs are cooked, remove pan from heat.
- Add egg mixture to the pan, stirring to prevent sticking.
- Use a fork or a whisk to stir a little water or milk into the raw eggs.

Peanut Butter and Jelly Sandwich
- Choose the kind of jelly you want to use.
- Spread peanut butter on one piece of bread.
- Put the slices of bread together with the peanut butter and jelly sides facing each other.
- First, take two pieces of bread from a loaf.
- Spread jelly on the other piece of bread.

A. How to Make Scrambled Eggs

1. _____
2. _____
3. _____
4. _____
5. _____

B. How to Make a Peanut Butter and Jelly Sandwich

1. _____
2. _____
3. _____
4. _____
5. _____

1 ▶ Summarizing Rules

Skill 1.2

Exercise 4

Critical Thinking

Think of a game you know how to play well, such as tic-tac-toe, baseball, chess, or a video game. A friend of yours has never heard of the game and wants to learn it. Summarize the rules and the best strategy for your friend.

_____

_____

_____

_____

_____

_____

_____

_____

_____

_____

_____

_____

_____

_____

_____

_____

_____

_____

_____

_____

Name _____ Date _____

 2 ▸ **Planning a Book**
Skills 2.1–2.3

You are writing a book based on the life of your best friend, whose name is Pasha.

A. Fill in the missing parts of the table of contents for this book.

Table of Contents

Chapter 1: Birth to Age 2

Chapter 2: _____

Chapter 3: Age 6 to 8

Chapter 4: Age 9 to 11

Chapter 5: _____

Chapter 6: Age 15 to 17

B. Circle the word or words that best complete each sentence. Refer to the chapter titles, if necessary.

1. *The Life of My Best Friend, Pasha* would be a good _____ .

   table of contents entry   index entry   glossary entry   book title

2. You are writing about something Pasha did when he was 10. You are working on _____ .

   the glossary   Chapter 4   the index   Chapter 10

3. You write the following entries
   second grade   14
   soccer team   92
   spelling champ   39
   swimming lessons   51

   You are working on the _____ .
   captions   index   glossary   appendix

4. You include a photo of yourself and your friend. Under the photo you will write _____ .

   a glossary   an appendix   an index   a caption

C. Write a chapter about Pasha's life on a separate sheet of paper.

2 ▶ Using Chapter Titles

Skill 2.4

Here are some chapter titles from a book. Read the titles and answer the questions that follow.

Recipes from Mexico	Recipes from Russia
Recipes from Greece	Recipes from France
Recipes from Ireland	Recipes from Italy

1. What kind of a book do you think this is? _____

2. What would be a good title for the book? _____

3. Your friend Sean says he has a great recipe for Irish stew, but he cannot remember the spices that go in it. Which chapter would you use to find out the spices to use?

_____

4. Francesca gives you her favorite recipe for Italian meatballs. You try it, but you do not like it. Which chapter would you use to find a better recipe for Italian meatballs?

_____

5. You go to a Mexican restaurant and order tamales, which you have never tried before. You like them so much you want to make them yourself. In which chapter might you find a recipe?

_____

6. Where would you find a recipe for Russian bean soup?

_____

7. You cannot remember if Greek salad uses feta cheese or Romano cheese. In which chapter would you look?

_____

8. You have lots of onions, so you decide to make a French onion soup. In which chapter might you find a recipe?

_____

Name _____ Date _____

Read each set of facts below. Then divide each circle into a pie graph that shows the facts.

1. Lee teaches English as a Second Language in night school. Each night he teaches a different group. The total number of students in his classes is 100. Here is a breakdown of Lee's class.

   - 25 from Russia
   - 25 from El Salvador
   - 20 from Guatemala
   - 20 from Mexico
   - 10 from Iran

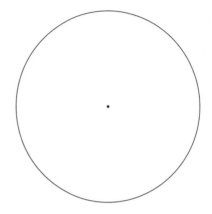

2. Anthony's Pet Store has 100 animals for sale. Here is a breakdown of the animals.

   - 50 fish
   - 25 dogs
   - 10 cats
   - 5 rabbits
   - 10 birds

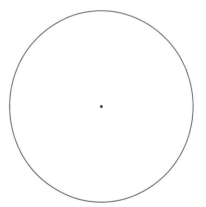

3. Kristine has $100 to spend on a party. She spends it on the following things.

   - Appetizers—$25
   - Soft drinks—$25
   - Desserts—$25
   - Decorations—$12.50
   - Door prizes—$12.50

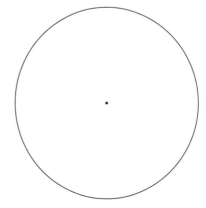

Name_____ Date_____

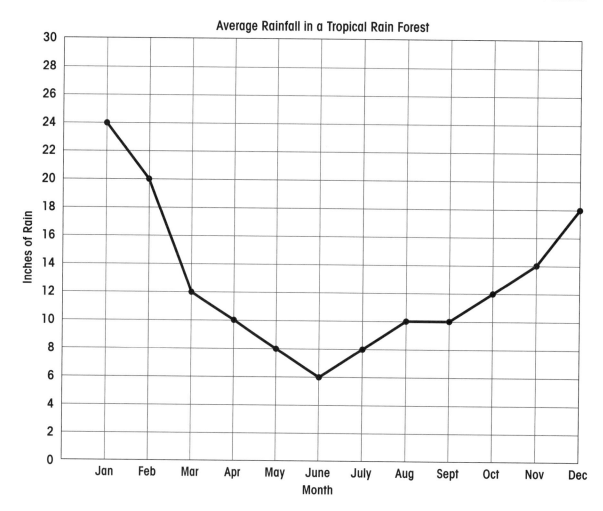

A. **Study the line graph. Then answer the questions.**

   1. Which month has the highest average rainfall? _____

   2. Which month has the lowest average rainfall? _____

   3. About how many inches of rain fall in August? _____

   4. About how many inches of rain fall in February? _____

B. **Write two questions of your own based on the line graph. Use a separate sheet of paper.**

3 ▶ Using the Dewey Decimal System

Skills 3.1–3.3

Exercise 9

Practice

The Dewey Decimal System divides nonfiction books in a library into 10 main numbered areas. These are listed in the box below.

Number Range	Subjects
000–099	General works (encyclopedias and similar works)
100–199	Philosophy (how people think and what they believe)
200–299	Religion (including mythology and world religions)
300–399	Social sciences (folklore, legends, government, manners and customs, vocations)
400–499	Language (dictionaries, grammar books)
500–599	Pure science (mathematics, astronomy, chemistry, nature study)
600–699	Technology (applied sciences—aviation, building, computer science, engineering, homemaking)
700–799	Arts (photography, drawing, painting, music, sports)
800–899	Literature (plays, poetry)
900–999	History (ancient and modern, geography, travel)

Write the number range in which you would find each of the following books.

1. A book explaining the religion of Islam _____

2. A book on Ansel Adams' photographs _____

3. A book on the philosophy of Bertrand Russell _____

4. A history of the ancient world _____

5. A Spanish-English dictionary _____

6. A vegetarian cookbook _____

7. A book on early astronomy _____

8. A book on Norse legends _____

9. The poetry of William Butler Yeats _____

10. Volume 11 of the *Encyclopaedia Britannica* _____

3 ▶ **Making Up Titles**   **Exercise 10**

Skills 3.1–3.3   *Critical Thinking*

A. Make up the title of a book that would be found in each of the main areas of the Dewey Decimal System. Look at the list in Exercise 9 for a description of each area.

  1. 000–099: _____

  2. 100–199: _____

  3. 200–299: _____

  4. 300–399: _____

  5. 400–499: _____

  6. 500–599: _____

  7. 600–699: _____

  8. 700–799: _____

  9. 800–899: _____

  10. 900–999: _____

B. The fiction area of a library does not have any Dewey decimal numbers. Instead, fiction is arranged alphabetically by the author's last name. Number the following list of fiction books in the order in which they would be found in a card catalog.

  _____ *Oliver Twist* by Charles Dickens

  _____ *To Kill a Mockingbird* by Harper Lee

  _____ *The Natural* by Bernard Malamud

  _____ *Sounder* by William Armstrong

  _____ *The Pearl* by John Steinbeck

  _____ *The Adventures of Huckleberry Finn* by Mark Twain

  _____ *I Know Why the Caged Bird Sings* by Maya Angelou

3 ▶ **Using a Dictionary**
Skill 3.4

A. Use a dictionary to find the meaning of each word in these sound-alike pairs. Write the definitions on the lines below.

1. seize and seas

_____

_____

2. sent and cent

_____

_____

3. gate and gait

_____

_____

4. pain and pane

_____

_____

5. rap and wrap

_____

_____

6. write and right

_____

_____

7. medal and meddle

_____

_____

B. On a separate sheet of paper, write three sound-alike pairs of your own. Give your sound-alike pairs to a classmate to explain their meanings.

3 ▶ Using Encyclopedias

Skill 3.5

Exercise 12

Practice

A. A set of encyclopedias is made up of books called volumes. The information in the box shows one way the volumes of an encyclopedia can be arranged. Use this information to answer the questions below.

Volume 1: A–B	Volume 6: K–L	Volume 10: S–T
Volume 2: C–D	Volume 7: M–N	Volume 11: U–V
Volume 3: E–F	Volume 8: O–P	Volume 12: W–X
Volume 4: G–H	Volume 9: Q–R	Volume 13: Y–Z
Volume 5: I–J		

1. Inéz wants to look up the history of the Hawaiian Islands. In which volume should she look? _____

2. Inéz is interested in fashion, especially jewelry. Which two volumes might be of interest to her? _____

3. When Inéz moved to Hawaii, she thought about taking up surfing. Which volume might tell her something about that sport? _____

4. After reading the book *Hawaii,* by James Michener, Inéz wanted to find out something about the author. In which volume would she find information? _____

5. When Mount Pinatubo erupted, Inéz began to wonder about the volcanoes in Hawaii. Which volume would give her information about volcanoes? _____

B. Use the information in the box to write the number of the volume in which you might find an article that will answer these questions.

1. Who is Jim Thorpe? _____

2. Who are some important figures in the history of photography? _____

3. What causes earthquakes? _____

4. What were the causes of World War I? _____

4 ▸ Taking a Test

Skills 4.1–4.2

A. Short Answer: Read the paragraphs below. Then answer the questions that follow.

> Sam Houston was elected governor of Texas in 1859. He had been a hero in the war for the independence of Texas from Mexico. His role in that war had made him the most popular person in Texas. Within two years, however, he was out of a job and no longer popular in his own state.
>
> Texas had become a state in 1845, largely because of Sam Houston's efforts. By 1861, however, most Texans wanted to join the South when the Civil War broke out. Houston was strongly against this idea. He said that Texas had joined the Union, not just the North or the South. In spite of Houston's arguments, the legislature of Texas voted 109 to 2 to join the South. Sam Houston refused to swear to be true to the new confederacy. Because of this, he was removed from his position as governor.

1. When was Sam Houston elected governor of Texas? _____

_____

2. Why had Sam Houston been so popular in 1859? _____

_____

3. What made him lose his popularity by 1861? _____

_____

B. Multiple Choice: Use the information from the paragraphs above to complete each sentence. Circle the letter of the correct ending.

1. Sam Houston was a hero in Texas's fight against _____ .

    a. France   **b.** Mexico   **c.** Spain   **d.** the North

2. Texas voted to join the South in _____ .

    a. 1845   **b.** 1859   **c.** 1861   **d.** 1865

3. Sam Houston was governor for _____ .

    a. 5 years   **b.** 10 years   **c.** 15 years   **d.** 2 years

C. On a separate sheet of paper, make up one short-answer question and one multiple-choice question based on the paragraphs above. Give them to a classmate to answer.

Name_____ Date_____

4 ▶ **Writing Test Questions**
Skill 4.3

Read each paragraph below. Then write sample test questions for each one. Be sure that the questions can be answered based on the paragraphs. (You do not have to write the answers.)

Paragraph A:

The Maya civilization was one of the great ancient civilizations of the Western Hemisphere. This culture expanded for more than 600 years in the rain forests of southern Mexico and Central America from about A.D. 250 to about A.D. 900. The Maya accomplished many things, including a 365-day calendar and a written language. They also produced beautiful temples and the mathematical idea of zero.

---

1. Write a true-false question based on the paragraph. _____

_____

2. Write a multiple-choice question based on the paragraph. _____

_____

3. Write a short-answer question based on the paragraph. _____

_____

Paragraph B:

Margaret Mee (1909–1989) was an English artist who lived in Rio de Janeiro, Brazil. Beginning in 1956, she traveled down the Amazon River 15 times, sketching and painting as she went along. Her finished art was published in two books: *Flowers of the Brazilian Forests* and *Flowers of the Amazon*. These paintings gave scientists their first look at the beautiful flowers of the rain forests of South America.

---

1. Write a true-false question based on the paragraph. _____

_____

2. Write a multiple-choice question based on the paragraph. _____

_____

3. Write a short-answer question based on the paragraph. _____

_____

Name _____ Date _____

4 ▶ Practicing Essay Tests

Skill 4.3

Exercise 15

Practice

A. Choose one of the topics in the box. Summarize what you know about it in a short essay.

baseball	football	tennis	your favorite sport
babysitting	a balanced diet	Internet	your favorite game
CDs	your favorite pet	hairstyles	modern music

_____

_____

_____

_____

_____

_____

B. Choose one of the pairs of topics in the box. Compare and contrast the two items in a brief essay.

sweaters and jackets	TV and computers	baseball and hockey
reggae and rap	cars and bicycles	ponytails and braids
Web surfing and reading a newspaper	guitar and piano	CD-ROM games and outdoor games

_____

_____

_____

_____

_____

Name_____ Date_____

4 ▶ Writing Directions

Skill 4.4

Exercise 16

Critical Thinking

Write a short essay about the best way to prepare for and take a test in school. Include the ideas listed in the box and put them in the correct order. You may have other tips of your own that you would like to add. Be sure to use complete sentences in your essay.

Read and review your notes. Study for short periods at a time. Study with a partner or a small group. Take notes on what you read while studying. Remember that a good guess is better than no answer on a multiple-choice test. Read questions carefully. Study when you are rested and alert. Look for words such as *always, never, not,* and *except* in the question. Look for direction words, such as *summarize* and *analyze.* Start studying early.

_____

_____

_____

_____

_____

_____

_____

_____

_____

_____

_____

_____

_____

_____

_____

Name _____ Date _____

 5 ▸ **Identifying Facts and Opinions**   **Exercise 17**

Skill 5.1   *Practice*

A. Read each of the following statements. If it is a fact, write *fact* on the line. If it is an opinion, write *opinion* on the line.

1. This short-haired white cat is named Waikiki. _____

2. Arielle could not say "white kitty." _____

3. Waikiki is a terrific name for a cat. _____

4. This cat is no trouble at all. _____

5. Waikiki does not like any food with liver in it. _____

6. We should not cater to this cat's tastes. _____

7. There is nothing worse than a spoiled cat. _____

8. No home should be without a cat. _____

9. Cats are much better pets than dogs. _____

10. Dogs bark. _____

11. Cats purr. _____

12. Purring is better than barking. _____

13. Waikiki eats one can of cat food per day. _____

14. Waikiki weighs 14 pounds. _____

15. Waikiki is too fat. _____

B. Write two facts and two opinions about dogs.

_____

_____

_____

_____

_____

_____

Name_____ Date_____

5 ▶ Conducting an Interview

Skills 5.1–5.2

Exercise 18

Critical Thinking

A. Find an ad that appeals almost entirely to people's emotions. Some good
subjects are perfume, toothpaste, soap, and shampoo ads. On the lines below,
explain how you know the ad appeals to emotions rather than to reason
and intelligence.

_____

_____

_____

_____

_____

_____

B. You have a chance to interview the manufacturer of the product in Part A.
What will you ask? What do you think the manufacturer will say? Write your
interview below. Continue writing on a separate sheet of paper, if necessary.

You:

_____

Manufacturer:

_____

You:

_____

Manufacturer:

_____

You:

_____

Manufacturer:

_____

Name_____ Date_____

5 ▶ Writing Ad Copy

Skill 5.2

Exercise 19

Critical Thinking

A. You have a dog, and she just had five puppies. You must give these puppies away to good homes, and you decide to write an ad. Write lists of words or phrases you could use to describe them. Put each word or phrase under the correct heading.

Facts   Opinions

_____   _____

_____   _____

_____   _____

_____   _____

_____   _____

_____   _____

_____   _____

B. Write an ad for a good home for the puppies. Use words and phrases from your lists above.

_____

_____

_____

_____

_____

_____

_____

_____

5 ▶ **Completing a Venn Diagram**   **Exercise 20**

Skill 5.2   *Practice*

A. Find two different toothpaste ads. Write the slogans and most important lines from each ad.

Ad 1:

_____

_____

Ad 2:

_____

_____

B. Complete the Venn diagram below. On the right and left sides, write the ideas that are different for each ad you chose for Part A. In the middle section, write the ideas that both ads have in common.

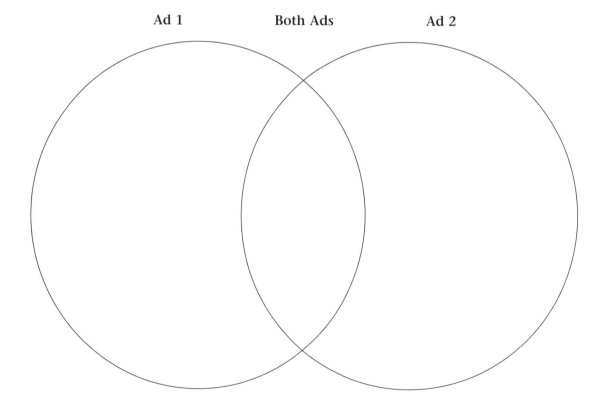

Ad 1   Both Ads   Ad 2

6 ▶ Identifying the Source   Exercise 21

Skill 6.1   *Practice*

A. Read each of the items below. Write where the information probably came from. Choose from these sources: *warranty, package label, price tag, care manual, instruction manual, estimate.*

1. Calories: 25; Protein: 1 g; Carbohydrate: 6 g _____

2. As Is _____

3. Estimated cost of repair: $239 _____

4. You will find that your gas grill will work better and you will enjoy using it more if you follow these instructions. _____

5. For one year from date of purchase, Nickels Grills will repair this Nifty Gas Grill, free of charge, if defective in material or workmanship. _____

6. Size 8/$48 _____

7. If you record a greeting longer than 16 seconds, the unit will sound three beep tones as a warning. If you hear these tones, repeat Steps 2 through 4. _____

B. Read each problem. Then answer the question.

1. Shirelle buys a $90 dress and wears it 30 times before she gets tired of it. Not counting dry cleaning costs, how much did each wearing cost? _____

2. Flora buys a dress for $45 and wears it 5 times. Not counting dry cleaning costs, how much did each wearing cost? _____

3. Which is a better buy per ounce: 12 ounces for 84¢ or 9 ounces for 81¢? _____

4. Alex tries on a $250 suit that really looks great. Then he tries on two $125 suits that look okay but not great. He can't decide what choice to make. List one pro and one con for each.

Two $125 Suits		One $250 Suit	
Pro	Con	Pro	Con
_____	_____	_____	_____

Name_____   Date_____

Read this limited warranty. Answer the questions that follow.

> Banana Corporation of America (BCA) warrants this product against defects in material or workmanship, as follows:
>
> 1. For a period of one year from the date of purchase, BCA will pay the labor charges of your BCA authorized service facility to repair the defective product.
>
> 2. BCA will supply, at no charge, new or rebuilt replacements for defective parts for a period of one year from the original date of purchase.
>
> 3. To obtain warranty service, you must take the product, or deliver the product prepaid, to a BCA authorized service facility.
>
> 4. This warranty does not cover cosmetic damage and damage due to accident, misuse, abuse, or negligence to the product including the antenna. This warranty is valid only in the United States of America.

1. Morris bought his VCR on May 14, 1999. On May 15, 2000, it broke. Who has to pay for repairs?

   _____

2. It will cost Morris $22 to ship the VCR to an authorized service facility. Will BCA pay for that? Explain.

   _____

3. Four months after Manuel bought his TV, the color turned to shades of blue. Does BCA have to give him new parts? Explain.

   _____

4. Renée accidentally dropped a barbell on her CD player. Now she says the CD player is "defective." Do you think BCA will agree with her? Explain.

   _____

5. Jaime's cat knocked over some nail polish on the stereo. The nail polish remover made the cabinet a different color. Will BCA fix it free of charge? Explain.

   _____

6 ▶ Recognizing Consumer Vocabulary   Exercise 23

Skill 6.1   *Practice*

**Read each description below of a product or service. Then circle the best ending
for each sentence. Explain whether the description is from an advertisement or
a label.**

1. Vitamin A, Vitamin C, Percent of U.S. RDA, Carbohydrate, Ingredients, Citric Acid,
Milligrams, Sodium Tripolyphosphate
These words would be used for _____ .

a carpet cleaning service   canned food   a bakery

Advertisement or label? _____

2. 100% Wool, 100% Cotton, Linen, Rayon, Polyester, Dry Clean Only, Hand Wash in
Cold Water, Size $14\frac{1}{2}$, One Size Fits All
These words would be used for _____ .

a restaurant   furniture   clothing

Advertisement or label? _____

3. All You Can Eat, Sizzling, Juicy, Baked, Grilled to Perfection, Beverages, Salad Bar
These words would be used for _____ .

a restaurant menu   an electronics store   a lighting store

Advertisement or label? _____

4. Safe, Durable, Educational, Fun, Hours of Entertainment, Eye-Hand Coordination,
Ages Five and Up
These words would be used for _____ .

housing   children's clothing   toys

Advertisement or label? _____

5. Trim, Tone, Reduce, Body Building, Aerobic Exercise, Free Weights, Steam Room,
Initiation Fee, Low Monthly Rates
These words would be used for _____ .

a gym   a doctor's office   a health food store

Advertisement or label? _____

6. USDA Select Beef, White Rose Potatoes, Longhorn Cheese
These words would be used for _____ .

a bookstore   a supermarket   a hardware store

Advertisement or label? _____

Name_____ Date_____

6 ► Offering a Recommendation

Skills 6.2–6.3

Exercise 24

Critical Thinking

Read each item. Write your advice and then give a reason for it.

1. Gayle has two small children, one big dog, and two medium-sized cats. She sees a white couch on sale for $200. She could get the same couch in dark green for $300. What is your advice?

   _____

   _____

2. Selena followed the directions for how to wash her new sweater. It shrank, and the color faded. What is your advice?

   _____

   _____

3. Mandy tries on a pair of jeans. They are a little too tight, but she plans to lose weight over the next two weeks. The jeans are on sale. What is your advice?

   _____

   _____

4. Michael's phone bill is very high. He sees some long-distance calls to Paris, Miami, and Toronto listed on it. He does not know anybody in any of those cities. What is your advice?

   _____

   _____

5. Anne-Marie bought an expensive clock from a clock store. It is supposed to chime every hour, but it does not. What is your advice?

   _____

   _____

6. Alex is making a stew that calls for a pinch of mustard seed. Mustard seed costs $3.59 for a small bottle, and Alex is on a budget. What is your advice?

   _____

   _____

Name_____ Date_____

7 ▶ Practicing Interviews

Skill 7.1

Exercise 25

Critical Thinking

Read each job ad below. In each case, you feel that you are qualified and you want the job. You will go for a job interview. Write two questions you think you might be asked. Then write the answers you would give.

> Dental Asst. Exp. only. X-ray lic req. F/t Call Jake: 555-7394.

1. Question:

_____

2. Answer:

_____

3. Question:

_____

4. Answer:

_____

> Retail sales. Antiques store seeks p/t sales help. Weekends nec. $8/hr. Some exp. req. 415-555-8723.

5. Question:

_____

6. Answer:

_____

7. Question:

_____

8. Answer:

_____

Name _____ Date _____

7 ▶ Reading Yellow Page Ads

Skill 7.2

Exercise 26

Practice

The two ads below might appear in the yellow pages of your phone book. Read each one and answer the questions that follow.

1. Juan is a student who wants a weekend job. He has a good bicycle, and he likes to go to the store. Which company would be best for him? _____

2. Elyse needs to hire a temporary file clerk for her busy office. Which company should she call? _____

3. Jorge applies for work at Todd's Temporaries. The next day, Todd sends him to a local office to do some typing. Will Jorge have to pay a fee to Todd? _____

4. Stuart calls Todd's Temporaries to get some help in his accounting department. Will Stuart have to pay a fee to Todd? _____ How do you know? _____

5. What does "Equal Opportunity Employer" mean?

   _____

6. Duane works for Todd's Temporaries. If he works full time, about how many checks can he expect each month? _____ How do you know? _____

7 ▶ Interpreting Classified Ads

Exercise 27

Skill 7.2

Practice

Read these classified ads. Answer the questions that follow.

> Cook with professional exp. For large groups.
> Flex. hours. Berkeley. 510-555-5400.

1. Carmen has been cooking for his family of ten children. Does he qualify for this job?

   _____ How do you know? _____

2. Mandy wants to work Monday through Friday from 5 P.M. to 9 P.M. Is this a good job

   for her? _____ How do you know? _____

> Driver's Helper. Clean driving record. Neat
> appear. Lift 75 lbs. p/t Apply at 1450 Oak
> Street, Chicago. See David.

3. Woody wants to work full time. Should he apply? _____ Why or why not?

   _____

4. Sam has no driver's license. Do you think David will hire him? _____ Why or

   why not? _____

5. Sarah weighs 100 pounds. Do you think she could do this job? _____ Why or

   why not? _____

> Receptionist. Hvy phones, med ofc exp.
> Call 555-3967.

6. Pablo likes to work outdoors. Is this a good job for him? _____ Why or why not?

   _____

7. Farhad does not like to talk on the phone, but he enjoys meeting people face to face.

   Is this a good job for him? _____ Why or why not? _____

7 ▶ Writing Your Own Ads

Exercise 28

Skill 7.3

Critical Thinking

Read each problem. Write an ad to solve it.

1. You work in an office in which the filing is piling up. You cannot get to it because you have too much typing to do. Your boss tells you to hire a temporary file clerk.

   _____

   _____

2. You go to school full time, and you want to get a job working about 20 hours a week.

   _____

   _____

3. Your grandmother lives in your house, and she has trouble getting around. You want to hire someone to be a companion and read to her for a few hours every afternoon.

   _____

   _____

4. You are looking for part-time work in your own neighborhood. You would like to help people with household, gardening, and shopping chores.

   _____

   _____

5. You are trying to decide if you should become a nursery school teacher, but you are just not sure you have enough patience. You would like to try the job out as a school aide.

   _____

   _____

6. You play the piano well. You would like to teach children to play, too. You are available evenings and weekends.

   _____

   _____

Name _____   Date _____

8 ▷ Choosing the Best Sentence

Skills 8.1–8.3

Exercise 29

Practice

Circle the sentence that would work best on a résumé. Explain why you chose that one.

1. My duties included feeding the animals.
   Fed 50 dogs, 40 cats, and 35 birds daily.
   I was responsible for feeding dogs, cats, and birds.

   _____

2. I helped the teacher on the playground.
   The children and I played together every day.
   Led 23 preschoolers in playground games.

   _____

3. Delivered medical supplies to 14 area hospitals.
   I drove the delivery truck and unloaded it.
   My last job was as a delivery person for a medical supplier.

   _____

4. Worked in a bakery selling bread, pies, cookies, and such.
   I was a counter person in a local bakery.
   Filled orders for baked goods at an average of 35 per hour.

   _____

5. Sorted and delivered mail to 86 employees twice a day.
   I worked in the mail room sorting and delivering the mail.
   My duties included the sorting and delivering of mail.

   _____

6. I worked as a gardener.
   Performed gardening chores for people in my neighborhood.
   Mowed lawns and trimmed hedges for 40 clients a week.

   _____

7. Assisted library patrons and reshelved books.
   Worked in a library after school.
   The librarian asked me to do many things.

   _____

8 ▶ Proofreading Résumés

Skill 8.4

These phrases might be found on a résumé. Each one has at least one spelling error. Circle the error or errors, and write the phrase correctly. Use a dictionary, if necessary.

1. Gradated from Morrison High School

_____

2. Worked after school at a local bakry

_____

3. Delivered newspappers for eight years

_____

4. Volenteered to work at a hospital

_____

5. Assissted the elderly with baths and meales

_____

6. Ran erands for people in the nieghborhood

_____

7. Dezigned and created stage setts for school plays

_____

8. Soled clothing in a department store durring the summer

_____

9. Meashured posters for a framming shop

_____

10. Sweppt the floor in a barber shop

_____

11. Stokked the shelves in a gardenning supply shop

_____

8 ▶ Evaluating Job Applications

Skill 8.5

Exercise 31

Critical Thinking

Read the information in the box and answer the questions below.

> It is against the law (Title VII of the Civil Rights Act of 1964) to refuse to hire someone because of race, color, religion, national origin, marital status, or sex. It is against the law (Age Discrimination in Employment Act of 1967) to refuse to hire someone because they are over 40. It is against the law (Americans with Disabilities Act of 1990) to refuse to hire someone because of disabilities that will not affect job performance. An employer is entitled to know if an applicant has been convicted of a crime, but not if he or she has ever been arrested.

1. A question on a job application asks for your date of birth. Do you have to answer that? _____ Explain. _____

2. A question on a job application for a restaurant asks if you are over 21. Do you have to answer that? _____ Explain. _____

3. A question on a job application asks if you have ever been arrested. Do you have to answer that? _____ Explain. _____

4. A question on a job application asks how much you weigh. Do you have to answer that? _____ Explain. _____

5. A question on a job application asks if you'd have a problem lifting 50-pound packages. Do you have to answer that? _____ Explain. _____

6. A question on a job application asks if you are married. Do you have to answer that? _____ Explain. _____

7. A question on a job application asks what year you graduated from high school. Do you have to answer that? _____ Explain. _____

8. A question on a job application asks if you graduated from high school. Do you have to answer that? _____ Explain. _____

9. A question on a job application asks for your religion. Do you have to answer that? _____ Explain. _____

Name_____ Date_____

8 ▶ Writing a Cover Letter

Skill 8.6

You see an ad for a job as an assistant chef at Tony's Vegetarian Restaurant, at 4000 Maple Drive, Jackson, CA 90000. It is a job you are qualified for. Write a cover letter to the manager, Tony Milano, telling him that you are enclosing a résumé. Write anything else you think he should know about you.

_____

_____

_____

_____

_____

_____

_____

_____

_____

_____

_____

_____

_____

_____

_____

_____

_____

_____

9 ▶ Preparing for an Interview

Skill 9.1

Exercise 33

Critical Thinking

A. You are getting ready to interview someone for a job. You are looking for a person to watch your house and take care of your pets while you go on vacation. Write a list of five questions that you will ask.

1. _____

   _____

2. _____

   _____

3. _____

   _____

4. _____

   _____

5. _____

   _____

B. Now you are the person being interviewed. Write the best answer to each of the questions in Part A.

1. _____

   _____

2. _____

   _____

3. _____

   _____

4. _____

   _____

5. _____

   _____

9 ▶ Offering Advice

Skills 9.1–9.3

Exercise 34

Critical Thinking

Read the paragraphs below. Write some advice for each person.

1. Rudolfo has a job interview in the morning. He decides to stay out late and have some fun. That way, he will be relaxed and in a good mood for the interview.

    Your advice: _____

    _____

2. Rosita's hair is tangled and dirty. Her job interview is in three hours.

    Your advice: _____

    _____

3. Jeremy is very nervous during his interview. He crosses his legs and swings the top one back and forth. He is afraid to look the interviewer in the eye.

    Your advice: _____

    _____

4. When asked about his weaknesses, Anthony says that he would rather play baseball than work.

    Your advice: _____

    _____

5. When asked about her strengths, Shawna says she could run the whole company by herself. She says she was the best worker at all 14 jobs she had in the past year.

    Your advice: _____

    _____

6. When asked why she should be hired, Luisa says that if she does not get a job soon, she will lose her apartment. Then she asks, "Do you want that to happen?"

    Your advice: _____

    _____

7. During the interview, Akbar asks, "How much paid vacation time will I get?"

    Your advice: _____

    _____

9 ▶ Choosing Correct Information   Exercise 35

Skills 9.1–9.3   *Practice*

Choose the word or words that best complete each sentence. Use context clues to help you. Write the answer on the line.

1. Kareem has an appointment to meet a possible employer. He will tell the employer

    about himself. Kareem is going on _____ .

    a vacation   a work shift   an interview

2. Suzanne uses expressions such as "cool," "right on," and "far out." She should not

    use such _____ during a job interview.

    silliness   slang   rudeness

3. The people who work with Lainie don't really like her. These _____ say she
    is lazy and bossy.

    parents   co-workers   enemies

4. Jared has always admired Eric and would like to be just like him. You might say that

    Eric is Jared's _____ .

    role model   half brother   employer

5. Tatiana goes to school during the day. She would like to work about 15 hours a week

    to earn spending money. She is looking for a _____ job.

    full-time   one-day   part-time

6. Ben says that he knows a lot about computers, cars, and cooking. He also says he is
    dependable, willing to learn, and easy to get along with. The employer probably has

    asked Ben about his _____ .

    habits   strengths   hobbies

7. Daria says that she worked as a playground aide after school. She also says that she
    volunteered to help second graders with their homework in a special library program.

    Daria is telling about her _____ .

    experience   plans   dreams

Name_____ Date_____

Each person mentioned in Exercise 35 has just been on a job interview. Write a follow-up letter for one of them. Make up information, such as the interviewer's name and company, and the person's last name and address. Thank the interviewer for seeing you, and state that you look forward to hearing from him or her.

_____

_____

_____

_____

_____

_____

_____

_____

_____

_____

_____

_____

_____

_____

_____

_____

_____

_____

10 ▶ Using the Employee Handbook

Skill 10.1

Exercise 37

Practice

Here is the table of contents of an employee handbook. Use the information to
answer the questions below.

1. Ike has an infant daughter. His wife's employer will not let her bring the child to
   work. Can Ike bring the child to his job?

   To find the answer, he should turn to page _____ .

2. Samantha's old gym just closed down. Can she use the company gym after work and
   during lunchtime?

   To find the answer, she should turn to page _____ .

3. Leah's boss has been making remarks that make her uncomfortable. If she reports
   him, will the company do anything about it?

   To find the answer, she should turn to page _____ .

4. Lars wants a raise, but he does not know how often the company gives raises.

   To find the answer, he should turn to page _____ .

5. Fiona has had the same doctor for 10 years, and she does not want to go to a clinic.
   She wants to know if the insurance on her new job covers visits to private doctors
   and if her doctor is in the plan's network.

   To find the answer, she should turn to page _____ .

6. Gabriel wants to know if he can wear running shoes to work.

   To find the answer, he should turn to page _____ .

Name_____ Date_____

10 ▶ Writing a Diary Entry

Skills 10.1–10.2

Exercise 38

Critical Thinking

Kevin made six mistakes during his first two days on the job. On Monday, his mistakes involved the following items: his clothing, his lunch break, and his morning break. On Tuesday, his mistakes involved his afternoon break, his starting time, and his finishing time. If he had read the employee handbook, he would have avoided them. Write diary entries Kevin might have written about his first and second days on the job. Consider what he did wrong, what his boss said, and how Kevin felt about it.

Monday: _____

Tuesday: _____

10 ▶ Writing an Employee Handbook

Skills 10.1–10.2

Exercise 39

Critical Thinking

Get together with a small group. Discuss the kind of company you think people would be happy to work for. On a separate sheet of paper, list the name of the company and what it does. Make a list of working conditions, benefits, and policies that you would like to see for everyone. Then use your list to write chapters of an employee handbook. Divide the list so that each person in your group writes one chapter. Use the space below to write your chapter. You may need to continue on a separate sheet of paper.

Chapter Title: _____

_____

_____

_____

_____

_____

_____

_____

_____

_____

_____

_____

_____

_____

_____

_____

_____

10 ▷ Understanding Forms

Skills 10.3–10.4

Exercise 40

Practice

Use the W-4 form below to answer the questions.

- - - - - - - - - - - - - - Cut here and give form W-4 to your employer. Keep the top part for your records. - - - - - - - - -

Form **W-4** Department of the Treasury Internal Revenue Service	**Employee's Withholding Allowance Certificate** ▶ For Privacy Act and Paperwork Reduction Act Notice, see page 2.	**2001**

1 Type or print your first name and middle initial	Last name	**2** Your Social Security number

Home address (number and street or rural route)	**3** ☐ Single ☐ Married ☐ Married, but withhold at higher Single rate. **Note:** *If married, but legally separated, or spouse is a nonresident alien, check the Single box.*
City or town, state, and ZIP code	**4** If your last name differs from that on your Social Security card, check here. **You must call 1-800-772-1213 for a new card.** . . . ▶ ☐

5 Total number of allowances you are claiming (from line H above or from the worksheets on page 2 if they apply) .	**5**
6 Additional amount, if any, you want withheld from each paycheck	**6** $

7 I claim exemption from withholding for 2001, and I certify that I meet **BOTH** of the following conditions for exemption:
- Last year I had a right to a refund of **ALL** Federal income tax withheld because I had **NO** tax liability; **AND**
- This year I expect a refund of **ALL** Federal income tax withheld because I expect to have **NO** tax liability.

If you meet both conditions, write EXEMPT here . . . . ▶ **7**

Under penalties of perjury, I certify that I am entitled to the number of withholding allowances claimed on this certificate, or I am entitled to claim exempt status.

Employee's signature
(Form is not valid unless you sign it) ▶ _____ Date ▶ _____

8 Employer's name and address (Employer: Complete 8 and 10 only if sending to the IRS.)	**9** Office code (optional)	**10** Employer identification number

1. You were going to claim an extra amount from your earnings to be withheld. On which item number would you write this?

_____

2. The name on your social security card is different from the name you use. What do you do?

_____

3. You are not sure how many allowances to claim. What should you do?

_____

4. On which item line do you write the total number of allowances you are claiming?

_____

5. To enter *exempt* on your W-4 form, what conditions do you need to meet?

_____

11 ▶ Writing Job Aids

Skill 11.1

Exercise 41

Critical Thinking

If you were in each of the following situations, what would you do? Write a job aid to help yourself or the person who is hiring someone.

1. You just got a job answering phones for a radio station. People call in to request songs and to dedicate the songs to friends and family. You are supposed to identify the station, write down the request and the dedication, and thank the caller for calling. Write a job aid to help you remember what to say and do.

_____

_____

_____

_____

_____

2. You just got a job at a busy diner. You have to set and clear tables. You also have to replace the ketchup, mustard, sugar, salt, and pepper. In addition, you have to sweep the floors and take out the trash. Write a job aid so you won't forget anything.

_____

_____

_____

_____

_____

3. You have just hired someone to come to your home to do your laundry, including the ironing. Write a job aid explaining what you want the person to do.

_____

_____

_____

_____

_____

11 ▶ Using Job Aids

Skill 11.1

Exercise 42

Practice

You work in an office. Your job is to make sure everything is shut down for the night before you leave. Create a job aid by placing the tasks listed in the box in the order you would do them.

Turn off the lights just before you leave.

Check to see if everyone has left the office.

Refill paper in the copier and fax machines after everyone has left.

Lock the doors behind you when you leave.

Turn off your computer right away.

---

1. First you would

_____

_____

2. Next you would

_____

_____

3. After that, you would

_____

_____

4. Then you would

_____

_____

5. Finally, you would

_____

_____

11 ▶ Writing a Chart

Skill 11.2

You manage a store that is open Monday through Saturday from 9:00 A.M. to 9:00 P.M. Of your five employees, two work full time (40 hours a week), and three work part time (12 hours, 18 hours, and 24 hours each a week). The chart below shows schedules for Casi, one of the full-time employees, and Skip, one of the part-time employees. Finish it, by filling in the names and creating schedules for the other full-time employee and the other two part-time employees. Then answer the questions that follow.

Time	Monday	Tuesday	Wednesday	Thursday	Friday	Saturday
9:00 A.M.	Casi	Casi		Casi	Casi	Casi
10:00 A.M.						
11:00 A.M.						
12:00 NOON						Skip
1:00 P.M.			Skip			
2:00 P.M.						
3:00 P.M.						
4:00 P.M.		Skip				
5:00 P.M.						
6:00 P.M.						
7:00 P.M.						
8:00 P.M.						
9:00 P.M.						

1. What days and hours does Casi work? _____

2. What days and hours does Skip work (the 12-hour part-time employee)? _____

3. What days and hours does the other full-time person work? _____

4. What days and hours does the 18-hour part-time employee work? _____

5. What days and hours does the 24-hour part-time employee work? _____

11 ▶ Understanding Job Aids

Skill 11.2

A. Answer the questions about job aids below.

1. What are the different kinds of job aids? How are they used?

   _____

   _____

2. What are some things to remember when creating a job aid?

   _____

   _____

3. What are two good places to keep a job aid? Why?

   _____

   _____

B. Name three tasks that might require job aids. Explain what kind of job aid would be best for each.

1. _____

   _____

   _____

2. _____

   _____

   _____

3. _____

   _____

   _____

12 ▶ Dramatizing a Conversation

Skill 12.1

Exercise 45

Critical Thinking

A. Choose one of the following two problems. Write a conversation that Person 1 (the employee) might have with Person 2 (the employer, co-worker, or customer).

1. Jaime and Joel are supposed to clean up the shop together each night after closing time. It takes about 20 minutes because there are a lot of chores to be done. For the past week, Joel has been leaving when the shop closes. It takes Jaime 40 minutes to do the cleaning by himself. Jaime is determined to say something—either to the boss or to Joel.

2. Della works in a day-care center. One mother has been bringing in a sick child for the past two days. Now Della thinks her own throat is getting sore. Della does not think this is right. She is getting ready to speak up—either to the mother or to her boss.

Person 1: _____

_____

Person 2: _____

_____

Person 1: _____

_____

Person 2: _____

_____

Person 1: _____

_____

Person 2: _____

_____

B. With a partner, take on roles and act out the conversation you wrote. Make any changes you think would improve it. Perform it for the class.

Name_____ Date_____

Pascual manages a dry-cleaning shop that also does laundry. One of his best customers has just complained about a burn on one of his white shirts. The customer is angry and wants something to be done. Pascual does not want to lose the customer. The employee who burned the shirt has several excuses and really needs to keep the job. Write a paragraph for each person, stating his or her point of view.

Customer: _____

_____

_____

_____

_____

_____

Pascual: _____

_____

_____

_____

_____

_____

Employee: _____

_____

_____

_____

_____

12 ▶ Completing a Story

Skill 12.1

Exercise 47

Read the story starter below. Then write an ending for it. Include several conversations between Lindsey and her co-workers and between Lindsey and her boss.

> Lindsey's vacation was scheduled to start on July 1. She already had tickets and reservations for a two-week stay at Myrtle Beach. She was planning to meet her sister Brianna there.
>
> On June 18, Hector, one of Lindsey's co-workers, broke a leg. He was going to miss about four weeks of work. Lindsey's boss said she would have to change the dates of her vacation. He said no one else knew as much about Hector's job as she did. Lindsey called her travel agent, who told her they could change all the reservations. The only problem was that it would cost an extra $400. Lindsey asked Jack, a co-worker, what she should do. Jack told her that she should

_____

_____

_____

_____

_____

_____

_____

_____

_____

_____

_____

_____

_____

_____

_____

12 **Offering Advice** **Exercise 48**

Skill 12.1 *Practice*

Read each problem below. Write some advice on how to solve it.

1. Esmé works for a florist. A customer complains that all the flowers in an expensive arrangement died within three days. Esmé thinks it was because the woman did not water the arrangement. The woman says the flowers were too old to begin with. What is your advice to Esmé?

_____

_____

2. Ruben works as an auto mechanic. He has asked his boss for overtime hours several times. The boss always says she will put it on the schedule, but she forgets. Russell, Ruben's co-worker, gets all the overtime he wants. What is your advice to Ruben?

_____

_____

3. Natalia is the fastest cashier in a supermarket. She is paid $4 an hour less than Elena, and $3 an hour less than Sal. Natalia thinks she deserves a raise. She thinks she should be paid more than any other cashier. What is your advice to Natalia?

_____

_____

4. Hal is the newest employee in a fast-food place. Part of his job is to take out the trash. He thinks this job should be shared by all employees. He thinks he is too talented to waste his time taking out trash. What is your advice to Hal?

_____

_____

5. Caitlyn works part time selling tickets in a movie theater. She also goes to school. She likes to do homework when she is not busy at work. Her boss does not like that. He thinks it looks "unprofessional." What is your advice to Caitlyn?

_____

_____

13 ▶ Debating an Issue

Skill 13.1

Exercise 49

Critical Thinking

Choose one of the four points of view below about the best place to live. Circle it. Then write arguments in favor of your position. In your argument, consider some of the following issues: entertainment, places for children to play, schools and educational opportunities, doctors and hospitals, stores, air quality, jobs, transportation, and available housing.

1. It is better to live in a major city than in the suburbs.

2. It is better to live in the suburbs than in a major city.

3. It is better to live in a rural area than in a city.

4. It is better to live in a city than in a rural area.

_____

_____

_____

_____

_____

_____

_____

_____

_____

_____

_____

_____

_____

_____

_____

13 ▶ Taking a Survey

Skill 13.1

Exercise 50

Critical Thinking

Interview 10 people. Ask each person: *What do you consider the five most important things in a home?* Have them make their choices from the following list. Based on the results of your survey, number these items in order of importance.

_____ location

_____ number of bedrooms

_____ number of bathrooms

_____ friendly neighbors

_____ good roommates

_____ nice view

_____ good carpets and drapes

_____ price

_____ storage space

_____ garage

_____ yard

_____ pets OK

_____ close to schools

_____ close to public transportation

_____ close to work

_____ safe neighborhood

_____ large kitchen

_____ other (Name it.) _____

13 ▶ Matching Renters with Rentals

Exercise 51

Skills 13.1–13.2

Practice

A. Read the following classified ads for rentals. Answer the questions.

Ad 1:

> 2 br. 1 ba. unfrn. apt. Nr. bus lines. W/w cpt.,
> lndry. in building, cat OK. $575 mo., $350
> sec. dep. Available immediately 555-6386

Ad 2:

> Lg. br. in 4-br. frn. home. Share kit. and lndry.
> $250 mo. + 1/2 of util. No pets. 555-8304

Ad 3:

> Small 1-br., 1-ba. unfrn. cottage with lg. yd.
> and vegetable garden. Dog or cat OK. Price
> negotiable—trade for gardening? 555-1600

1. Can Jodie get the apartment described in Ad 1 if she has a roommate? _____ Why?

   _____

2. Jodie can afford $300 a month rent. She has a cat. Can she get the place described in

   Ad 2 on her own? _____ Why? _____

   _____

3. Jodie likes the sound of the home described in Ad 3. If Jodie is a good gardener, can

   she get a better deal on her rent? _____

   _____

B. Choose one of the ads. Rewrite it, spelling out the abbreviated words. Use a separate sheet of paper.

13 ▶ Writing How-to Directions

Skills 13.1–13.5

Exercise 52

Practice

Your pen pal from England has just arrived in this country. Your pen pal has always lived on a family farm and now wants to live in a city. Write directions for your pen pal on how to find a place to live. Include details about how to choose a neighborhood, how to read classified ads, and what to look for. Give tips on filling out applications and reading lease agreements. Explain any words you think your pen pal might need to know.

1. How to Find a Place to Live: _____

_____

_____

_____

2. How to Choose a Neighborhood: _____

_____

_____

_____

3. How to Read Classified Ads: _____

_____

_____

_____

4. What to Look For: _____

_____

_____

_____

5. Tips on Filling Out Directions: _____

_____

_____

_____

Name _____   Date _____

You live in San Carlos, California. You have tickets to the Stanford University/USC football game. It takes place at Stanford Stadium in Palo Alto on Saturday. Use the train schedules to plan your trip to the big game. Then answer the questions below.

Train Saturday Schedule – San Carlos to Palo Alto

San Carlos	6:45	8:45	10:45	**12:45**	**2:45**	**4:45**	**8:45**
Redwood City	6:49	8:49	10:49	**12:49**	**2:49**	**4:49**	**8:49**
Atherton	6:53	8:53	10:53	**12:53**	**2:53**	**4:53**	**8:53**
Menlo Park	6:56	8:56	10:56	**12:56**	**2:56**	**4:56**	**8:56**
Palo Alto	6:59	8:59	10:59	**12:59**	**2:59**	**4:59**	**8:59**

(times in bold are **P.M.**)

Train Saturday Schedule – Palo Alto to San Carlos

Palo Alto	6:28	8:28	10:28	**12:28**	**2:28**	**5:28**	**8:28**
Menlo Park	6:31	8:31	10:31	**12:31**	**2:31**	**5:31**	**8:31**
Atherton	6:34	8:34	10:34	**12:34**	**2:34**	**5:34**	**8:34**
Redwood City	6:38	8:38	10:38	**12:38**	**2:38**	**5:38**	**8:38**
San Carlos	6:42	8:42	10:42	**12:42**	**2:42**	**5:42**	**8:42**

(times in bold are **P.M.**)

1. The game begins at 2:00 P.M. You would like to be there an hour early. You decide to take the 12:45 P.M. train, which will arrive in Palo Alto at _____ P.M. How many minutes does the train ride take? _____

2. Your friend will be joining you on the train in Atherton. What time will your train arrive in Atherton? _____

3. The game is over at 5:30 P.M. You decide to eat dinner in Palo Alto. What time is the latest train going back to San Carlos? _____ When does it arrive in San Carlos? _____

4. Your friend takes the same train home. What time will he arrive in Atherton? _____

14 ▶ Interpreting a Map

Skill 14.3

Exercise 54

Practice

It is a beautiful Saturday in September. You and a friend decide to visit San Francisco. Use the map to answer the questions. Then draw a line on the map to show your route.

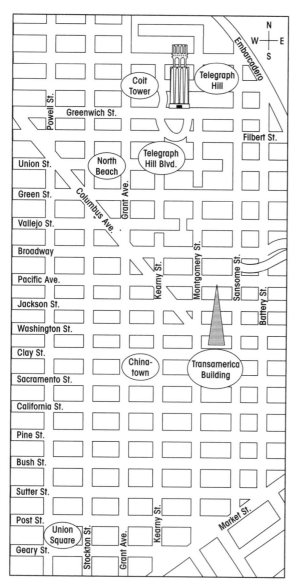

1. You and your friend get off the bus at the northernmost point of the Embarcadero. Which streets will lead you to the Transamerica Building?

   _____

   _____

2. Which street will you walk on to get from the Transamerica Building to Chinatown?

   _____

   _____

3. From Chinatown, you decide to go shopping at Union Square. Which streets will you use?

   _____

   _____

4. You want to have lunch in a restaurant in North Beach. From Union Square, how can you walk there?

   _____

   _____

5. Your last stop before the bus ride home is Coit Tower on Telegraph Hill. How can you get to Coit Tower from North Beach?

   _____

   _____

14 ▶ Interpreting Illustrated Signs

Skill 14.4

Exercise 55

Critical Thinking

The words in the box describe some international road signs. Write the meaning of each sign on the line below it.

CURVE	ROAD WORK	TUNNEL	PEDESTRIAN CROSSING
WATCH OUT FOR CHILDREN	ANIMAL CROSSING	ROAD NARROWS	SLIPPERY ROAD
NO U TURNS	NO LEFT TURN	PARKING	HOSPITAL
TELEPHONE	FILLING STATION	CAMPING SITE	

1. _____

2. _____

3. _____

4. _____

5. _____

6. _____

7. _____

8. _____

9. _____

10. _____

11. _____

12. _____

13. _____

14. _____

15. _____

14 ▶ Designing Signs

Skill 14.4

Some places need their own special signs. For example, Deer Crossing signs
will be found only on roads near deer habitats. Think about each problem
below. Design a sign to warn people about it. Use a picture, and add words if
you wish. Remember, your sign should be easy to understand. Draw your signs
in the boxes.

1. You own some land on which people
do target practice. They use bows and
arrows, shooting at targets that are
mounted on stands. You don't want
any hikers getting hurt. Design a sign
to warn them.

2. You are a forest ranger. There are
bears in your area, and you know
that people think they are cute.
You know, however, that bears are
dangerous. Design a sign warning
tourists not to feed the bears.

3. You work in a zoo. You see some
people teasing the elephants. The
people do not realize that they could
be hurt if the animals get angry.
Design a sign warning people to
leave the elephants alone.

4. You are a camp counselor. You take
groups of children on hikes. There is
a huge beehive in a tree along one of
the paths you use. The children are
curious about the honey. Design a
sign warning the children not to
try to taste the honey.

Name_____ Date_____

15 ► Filling out Checks

Skills 15.2–15.3

Exercise 57

Practice

A. Your name is David Martin. You go to Menendez Furniture Store on March 8, 2000 where you spend $102.50 buying tables for your home. Use this information to fill out the check below.

David Martin 100 4th St. Lily, CA 94000	$\frac{00/3214}{8654}$ NO. 1314

DATE _____

PAY TO THE
ORDER OF _____ $ [   ]

_____ DOLLARS

Bank of Lily
1173 Howe St.
Lily, CA 94000

MEMO _____   _____

⑆437 ⑈128142⑈

B. After you write the check, you remember the $1.50 check fee. You also remember that your account balance before you wrote the check was $750.00. Use this information and the information from the check that you filled out to complete the check register below.

		RECORD ALL CHARGES OR CREDITS THAT AFFECT YOUR ACCOUNT						
NUMBER	DATE	DESCRIPTION OF TRANSACTION	PAYMENT/DEBIT (−)	FEE (IF ANY) (−)	DEPOSIT/CREDIT (+)	BALANCE $		
			$	$	$			
		REMEMBER TO RECORD AUTOMATIC PAYMENTS/DEPOSITS ON DATE AUTHORIZED						

Name_____ Date_____

Read the following section of Ramona's credit card bill. Then answer the questions.

Previous Balance	Charges	Finance Charge	Credits/Returns
$117.78	$52.38	$1.76	$39.87

1. "Previous Balance" means the amount Ramona owed last month. How much was

   Ramona's previous balance? _____

2. "Charges" means new purchases made this month. How much did Ramona charge

   this month? _____

3. The "Finance Charge" is the interest charged on the balance. How much was the

   finance charge? _____

4. "Credits/Returns" refers to items that were brought back to the store for a refund.

   How much did Ramona get for a refund this month? _____

5. Add the charges and the finance charge to the previous balance. What is the total

   amount? _____

6. Now subtract the amount allowed for credit. What is the result? _____

7. Ramona made a payment last month of $50. How much does she owe now?

   (This is her new balance.) _____

8. If Ramona makes a payment of $82.05, will she owe anything for next month? Explain.

   (She does not use this credit card again.) _____

15 ▸ Debating an Issue

Skills 15.4–15.5

Exercise 59

Critical Thinking

Kyle wants to get a major credit card. He remembers that one time he did not
have enough cash in a restaurant to pay his bill. He had been embarrassed to
ask for a loan from his friend. Tracy tells Kyle that he should think twice about
getting a credit card. She remembers one time that her credit card payment used
up most of her paycheck. Write a conversation Kyle and Tracy might have about
this issue.

Kyle: _____

_____

_____

Tracy: _____

_____

_____

Kyle: _____

_____

_____

Tracy: _____

_____

_____

Kyle: _____

_____

_____

Tracy: _____

_____

_____

15 ▶ Planning a Commercial

Skills 15.4–15.5

You work for a consumer interest group. You have noticed that large numbers of people are wasting a lot of money by paying interest on credit cards. Write a TV commercial in which you tell people what else they can do with their money. Remind them about the true cost of credit cards. Describe your commercial below. Add any dialogue that is necessary.

Purpose of the Commercial: _____

_____

_____

_____

Setting of the Commercial: _____

_____

_____

_____

Characters in the Commercial: _____

_____

_____

_____

Dialogue in the Commercial: _____

_____

_____

_____

Final Words of the Commercial: _____

_____

_____

_____

16 ▶ Reading a Telephone Book

Skill 16.1

Exercise 61

Study this part of a phone book. Then answer the questions.

City of San Mateo

Libraries

    Main Branch, 55 W 3d Ave S Mto

        Hours: Mon.–Wed. 10–8 P.M.; Th. 10–6 P.M.

        Fri. 10–5 P.M.; Sat. 9–5 P.M.

        Sun. during School Year 1–4 P.M.

            All Departments 555-4680

            Administration 555-4685

            Reference 555-4684

    Hillsdale Branch, 205 W Hillsdale Blvd S Mto . . 555-4688

        Hours: Mon.–Tues. 1–9 P.M.; Wed.–Th. 10–6 P.M.

        Sat. 10–5 P.M.; Fri., Sun. Closed

    Marina Branch, 1530 Susan Ct S Mto 555-4686

        Hours: Mon.–Tues. 1–9 P.M.; Th. 10–6 P.M.

        Sat. 10–5 P.M.; Wed., Fri., Sun. Closed

---

1. How many branches does the San Mateo Library have? _____

2. Which branch is open the most hours? _____

3. It is a Sunday in August. Is any branch of the San Mateo Library open? _____

4. For a report, Alicia needs to know how long the Nile River is. She cannot find this

information in any book she has at home. Does she have to go to the library to find

out? Explain your answer. _____

5. Katie wants to know if the library has a copy of *In My Hands: Memories of a Holocaust*

Rescuer by Irene Gut Opdyke. List two ways she can find out. _____

_____

6. Melido usually uses the Marina Branch of the library because it is only a 15-minute walk

from his house. It is Tuesday night at 8:50. Can he walk over to check a fact? What

are two other choices? _____

_____

16 ▶ Using a Telephone Book

Exercise 62

Skill 16.1

Practice

Most telephone books are divided into white pages and yellow pages. Here are sample entries from each section.

From the White Pages:

Chim Chimney   1229 Meehan Dr. 555-3892

From the Yellow Pages:

Chimneys and Fireplaces

Sweeping	Dampers
Smoke Problems	Stoves and Inserts
Written Safety Inspections	Stove Pipes
Masonry Repairs	Spark Arrestors

Fully insured. Certified with National Chimney Sweep Guild and Independent Safety Commission.

CHIM CHIMNEY 555-3892 FAX #: 555-3998

Write a short essay in which you compare and contrast white pages and yellow pages of a telephone book. In your essay, consider questions such as: *What do both sections tell you? How are both sections arranged? How are the sections different from each other?* You may wish to look in a phone book for more ideas.

_____

_____

_____

_____

_____

_____

_____

_____

_____

16 ▶ Writing an Editorial

Skill 16.3

Exercise 63

Critical Thinking

Jordan has just transferred to a new school. On her first day, she learns that she has to wear a school uniform to classes every day. Jordan tells her friend Cole that she does not want to have to buy new clothes or be told what to wear. Cole tells Jordan that uniforms give everyone pride in the school. They also keep students from wasting money trying to compete with each other with trendy clothing. What do you think about school uniforms? Choose a side—pro or con. Write an editorial stating and defending your point of view.

_____

_____

_____

_____

_____

_____

_____

_____

_____

_____

_____

_____

_____

_____

_____

_____

_____

16 ▶ Writing an Essay

Skill 16.3

Here are three reasons why the government wants cars to be registered.

1. If someone stole your car and the police found it, they would know whose it was.

2. If someone crashed into your car and drove away, you could find the hit-and-run driver.

3. If you sold your car and it was involved in a bad accident, you could prove the car was no longer yours.

Think of at least three other reasons the government requires car registration. Write an essay or a story that shows why registering cars is a good idea.

_____

_____

_____

_____

_____

_____

_____

_____

_____

_____

_____

_____

_____

_____

_____

_____

Name_____ Date_____

17 ▶ Using Tax Forms

Skills 17.1–17.3

Exercise 65

Practice

Use the information in the W-2 form below to answer the questions.

a Control number			Void ☐	For Official Use Only	
b Employer identification number				**1** Wages, tips, other compensation $19,565.00	**2** Federal income tax withheld $1,600.50
c Employer's name, address, and ZIP code Hathaway Distributors 312 Margaretta Street Summit Station, PA 17979				**3** Social security wages $19,565.00	**4** Social security tax withheld $907.22
				5 Medicare wages and tips	**6** Medicare tax withheld
				7 Social security tips	**8** Allocated tips
d Employee's social security number 999-22-4623				**9** Advance EIC payment	**10** Dependent care benefits
e Employee's name (first, middle initial, last) Josh Moody 452 Revere Street Pottsville, PA 17901				**11** Nonqualified plans	**12** Benefits included in box 1
				13 See instr. for box 13	**14** Other
f Employee's address and ZIP code				**15** Statutory employee ☐ Deceased ☐ Pension plan ☐ Legal rep. ☐ Deferred compensation ☐	

16 State Employer's state I.D. no.	**17** State wages, tips, etc.	**18** State income tax $255.75	**19** Locality name	**20** Local wages, tips, etc.	**21** Local income tax

Form **W-2 Wage and Tax Statement 1999**   Copy B to be filed with employee's federal tax form   Dept. of Treasury—IRS

1. How much money did this person earn according to this W-2?

   _____

2. How much federal tax does this person have to pay?

   _____

3. What is this person's social security number?

   _____

4. How much will this person have to pay in state income tax?

   _____

5. Where was this person employed?

   _____

17 ▶ Interpreting Tax Rules

Skills 17.2–17.3

Exercise 66

Critical Thinking

Each of the following sentences explains a rule about who can use Form 1040EZ. Circle the best ending for each statement that follows the rule.

1. "Use this form if your filing status is single."
   This means that you *cannot* use the form if _____ .

   you have a sister or brother.   you are married.

   you have two children.   you live with anyone else.

2. "Use this form if you do not claim any dependents."
   This means that you *may be able* to use the form if _____ .

   you claim your children as dependents.   someone else claims you as
                                               a dependent.

   you claim your mother as a dependent.   you claim only yourself as a
                                               dependent.

3. "Use this form if you were under 65 at the end of 2000."
   This means that you *cannot* use the form if _____ .

   you are 72 years old.   you are under 65 years old.

   you are retired.   you are 56 years old.

4. "Use this form if your taxable income is less than $50,000."
   This means that you *cannot* use the form if _____ .

   your taxable income is over $50,000.   you gave $50,000 to charity.

   you earned over $50,000.   you earned less than $50,000.

5. "Use this form if you had only wages, salaries, tips, and taxable scholarship or fellowship grants, and your taxable interest income was $400 or less."
   This means that you *may be able to* use the form if _____ .

   your savings account interest was $98.50.   you earned royalties on a book.

   you made a profit when you sold your ring.   you inherited $6,000.

Name_____ Date_____

 17 ▶ **Reading a Tax Table**   **Exercise 67**

Skills 17.2–17.4   *Critical Thinking*

A. Read the tax rate table for single individuals. Then answer the questions
that follow.

If taxable income is:		The federal income tax is:	
Over—	But not over—		of the amount over—
$ 0	$20,350	$ 0 + 15%	$ 0
20,350	49,300	3,052.50 + 28%	20,350
49,300	—	11,158.50 + 31%	49,300

1. Lanie is a single woman. In 1999 her taxable income was $21,500. Her federal

   income tax was _____ of that.

2. Quinn is a single man who earned $23,350 in 1999. How much of his income was

   taxed at the rate of 15%? _____ How much was taxed at the rate of 28%? _____

   How much was taxed at the rate of 31%? _____

   Circle the amount you think Quinn had to pay.

   $560.00 $3,052.50 $3,892.50

3. If a single person earned $58,200 in 1999, how much of that will be taxed

   at 31%? _____

B. Use the tax rate table in Part A to make up three more word problems about
taxes. Exchange problems with a classmate and solve them.

_____

_____

_____

_____

_____

_____

17 ▶ Getting Tax Help

Skills 17.3, 17.5

Exercise 68

Practice

A. Write a paragraph explaining the benefits of reading tax instructions. What are some things that you might do incorrectly if you do not read the instructions? What are some things you might forget to do?

_____

_____

_____

_____

_____

_____

_____

_____

_____

B. Write a paragraph explaining the pros and cons of using a tax service. Why might you need help understanding your taxes?

_____

_____

_____

_____

_____

_____

_____

_____

_____

Name_____ Date_____

18 ▶ Finding Health Care
Skill 18.1

Exercise 69

Practice

A. Use each Yellow Pages index below to answer the questions that follow it.

Dentist–	Pages
Dental Services	370
Dentists	370–391
List arranged by specialty	391–392
List arranged by locality	392–395
Referral service	395

1. If you want to find the closest dentist to where you live, on what pages would

you look? _____

2. If you want to find a particular kind of dentist, on what pages would

you look? _____

Mental–	Pages
Health Services See	
Counselors-Licensed	
Professional	356–357
Marriage, Family, Child and	
Individual Counselors	687–689
Health Services	699–701
Retardation and Developmentally	
Disabled Services	701

3. On what pages would you look to find mental health services for

a child? _____

4. If you wanted help for someone with a mental disability, on what pages would you

look? _____

5. If you wanted to find a professional counselor, on what pages would

you look? _____

B. Describe a situation when you might ask a friend to help you find health care. Then describe a situation when you would use a telephone book to help you find health care. Write your answers on a separate sheet of paper.

18 ▶ Solving Problems   Exercise 70

Skill 18.2   *Practice*

Study the list of doctors and their specialties below. Then complete each sentence with the right doctor for each problem. Write the answer on the line.

Dermatologist (skin doctor)

Podiatrist (foot doctor)

Gastroenterologist (stomach, intestines, and liver doctor)

Hematologist (blood doctor)

Nephrologist (kidney doctor)

Pediatrician (baby and children's doctor)

Ophthalmologist (eye doctor)

Orthopedist (bone doctor)

---

1. Vicki broke her right arm when she was skiing. She will visit the _____ .

2. Something is wrong with Yolanda's blood. She has been going to the _____ .

3. Simon's eyesight seems to be getting a little blurry. He made an appointment with

the _____ .

4. Karl got kicked in the kidneys during a football game. His _____

says he will be okay.

5. Doreen has been having stomach pains. Her _____ gave her a prescription.

6. Greg's baby son needs to get his measles shots. Greg made an appointment with

the _____ .

7. Randall has been having trouble with acne and pimples. His _____

said it is very common.

8. Leeza's feet hurt after she stood in one place for three hours. She should see

her _____ .

18 Summarizing Information

Skill 18.3

Exercise 71

Critical Thinking

Read the following paragraphs. Then write a two-sentence summary of each one.

1. You have a greater chance of developing serious health problems if you are too heavy. Being too heavy is a common problem in the United States. This condition can cause high blood pressure, heart disease, stroke, the most common type of diabetes, some cancers, and other kinds of illnesses. Being too thin is a less common problem in the United States. It occurs with anorexia nervosa (a disease in which the victim starves herself—or, in rare cases, himself). It also is linked with osteoporosis (loss of calcium in the bones) in women.

   Summary:

   _____

   _____

   _____

   _____

   _____

2. Alzheimer's disease (AD) is an illness that affects the brain. It causes memory loss and dependence on others. It was named after Alois Alzheimer, a German doctor, who first described the disease. He had a 51-year-old female patient who suffered from memory loss, depression, and hallucinations (seeing and hearing things that are not really there). She also experienced confusion. That means she did not know where she was most of the time. After she died, doctors looked at her brain. It showed damage in certain parts, a condition now known to be typical in AD patients.

   Summary:

   _____

   _____

   _____

   _____

   _____

18 ▸ Reading a Medicine Label

Skill 18.4

Exercise 72

Critical Thinking

Read the medicine label below. Then answer the questions.

Indications: For the temporary relief of minor aches and pains associated with the common cold, headaches, toothache, muscle aches, backache, and arthritis, and for the reduction of fever.

Directions: *Adults*—Take 1 tablet every 4 to 6 hours while symptoms last. If pain or fever does not respond to 1 tablet, 2 tablets may be used, but do not exceed 6 tablets in 24 hours, unless directed by a doctor. The smallest effective dose should be used. Take with food or milk if occasional and mild upset stomach, stomach pain, or heartburn occurs with use. Consult a doctor if these symptoms are more than mild or if they last. *Children*—Do not give this product to children under 12 except under the advice and supervision of a doctor.

1. Meredith had a terrible headache, so she took two tablets. Now she has a terrible stomachache. What should she do now? _____

   _____

2. Philippe has a toothache, and his dentist cannot see him until tomorrow afternoon. He needs to get to sleep, but the pain is bothering him. How many tablets should he take? _____ What if the pain does not go away after half an hour? _____

   _____

3. Gino is eight years old, and he hurt his knee when he was playing. Should his mother give him one of these tablets? _____ Why? _____

   _____

4. Racquel gets a backache every day at about 4:00 P.M. She takes two tablets, and it goes away. It comes back the next day. This has been going on for two months. What is your advice to Racquel? _____

5. These tablets help Jordan's headache, but sometimes he gets a mild upset stomach when he takes them. What should he do? _____

19 ▶ Thinking About Fires

Exercise 73

Skill 19.1

Critical Thinking

A. Every year, thousands of people die in fires. If a fire suddenly broke out in your home, would you know what to do? Read the fire safety rules and then answer the questions.

In Case of Fire

Leave your home immediately.

Do not open a door that feels hot.

Crawl on the floor when going through a smoky room.

Drop and roll if your clothes catch on fire.

When you are safe, call the fire department.

---

1. Jeremy's house is on fire. He runs down the hall to get to a phone. He wants to call 911. Is he doing the right thing? _____ Explain. _____

_____

2. Tricia's jacket catches on fire. She starts to run toward the hose in her backyard. Is she doing the right thing? _____ What would you do? _____

_____

3. The living room of Lesley's house is full of smoke. What is the best way for her to get through the living room to reach the front door? _____

_____

B. What fire safety equipment do you have in your home? Describe where it is located.

_____

_____

_____

C. On a separate sheet of paper, draw a diagram of your home. Draw arrows to show escape routes for members of your family.

19 ▸ Writing a List

Skill 19.1

Exercise 74

Critical Thinking

You are responsible for the safety of a child in your home. The child is just about ready to start walking. Go through your home, room by room. Look for things that could be dangerous to this child. Make a list of those things. Write what you think should be done in each room to make it safe for the child. To get ideas, read the list of safety hazards in the box.

low electrical outlets	loose wires	low-silled open windows
unlined rugs	medicines without safety caps	uncovered cleaning supplies
glass objects on ledges	uncovered painting supplies	sharp tools
steep steps	knives on the floor	poisonous materials

1. Bedrooms: _____

_____

_____

2. Living room: _____

_____

_____

3. Kitchen: _____

_____

_____

4. Bathroom: _____

_____

_____

5. Other: _____

_____

_____

19 ▶ Interpreting Danger Words

Skill 19.2

Exercise 75

Study the pictures below. Then answer the questions that follow.

A

DANGER
COMBUSTIBLE

B

Not for
Internal
Use

C

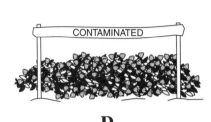

CONTAMINATED

D

1. Which picture warns you of the chance of explosion?

   _____

2. Which two pictures warn you to stay away?

   _____

3. Which picture warns you *not* to drink something?

   _____

4. You see fruit growing in the field shown in picture D. Should you pick them? Explain.

   _____

5. Where should you *not* store the item shown in picture B?

   _____

6. Why is it a good idea to wash your hands after handling the contents of the bottle shown in picture C?

   _____

7. It begins raining hard as you walk past the building in picture A. Is it all right to wait under the porch until the rain slows down? Explain.

   _____

19 ▶ Using a Chart

Skill 19.3

Exercise 76

Practice

Study the chart below. Then answer the questions that follow.

Skin type	For safe sun exposure time, use these sunscreens:		
	4 SPF*	8 SPF	15 SPF
Fair	10 minutes	40 to 80 minutes	$1\frac{1}{2}$ to 2 hours
Medium	50 to 80 minutes	2 to $2\frac{1}{2}$ hours	5 to $5\frac{1}{2}$ hours
Dark	$1\frac{1}{2}$ to 2 hours	$3\frac{1}{2}$ to 4 hours	all day

*SPF=Sun Protection Factor

1. What do the letters SPF stand for? _____

   _____

2. Geena's skin is a medium tone. She will be at a ball park for about five hours. Which

   sunscreen should she use? _____ Why? _____

   _____

3. Bryan has dark skin. He will be doing some gardening from noon until 4 P.M. What

   kind of sunscreen should he use? _____ If he has sunscreen with a 4 SPF, how

   many times will he have to apply it? _____ Explain. _____

   _____

4. Hans has very fair skin. He is at the beach with some friends. The only sunscreen

   anyone brought has a 4 SPF. How often will Hans have to apply it? _____

   _____

5. Lauren has fair skin. She used up the last of her sunscreen at 1:00 P.M. It had a

   15 SPF. At what time should she get out of the sun? _____

20 ▸ Using Headlines

Skill 20.1

Exercise 77

Critical Thinking

A. Read the following introduction to a magazine article. Then write three possible headlines for this article on the lines below.

> Al Jizah, Egypt—A team of American and Egyptian archaeologists made a stunning discovery on April 5. They unearthed three complete specimens of Stone Age humans who may have lived in the Nile delta region nearly 8000 years ago.
>
> "This is an amazing discovery," claims Dr. Michael Richmond, senior archaeologist and head of the digging team. There is evidence here that Stone Age people began gathering in villages sooner than we thought.

1. _____

2. _____

3. _____

B. Choose your best headline from Part A. Then write two more paragraphs on the lines below to complete the article. Continue your paragraphs on a separate sheet of paper if you need more room.

_____

_____

_____

_____

_____

_____

_____

_____

_____

20 ▸ Using a Newspaper Index

Skill 20.2

Exercise 78

Practice

Use the newspaper index below to answer the questions that follow.

INSIDE THE PAPER

Area News B1	Horoscope D9
Books D6	Obituaries E7
Business E1	People B8
Classified E12	Radio Listings D5
Comics D8	Sports C1
Crossword D7	TV Listings D7
Entertainment D1	Weather B10
Editorials A10	World Events A6

1. If you want to see a movie, in what section would you look?

   _____

2. You have an outdoor event planned for the weekend. In what section would you look to see if rain will cause you problems?

   _____

3. In what section would you look to see if the newspaper printed your letter to the editor?

   _____

4. In what section would you see the headline "New York Yankee Breaks Home Run Record"? Explain why.

   _____

5. In what section would you see the headline "European Leaders Travel To China"? Explain why.

   _____

6. In what section would you see the headline "Blues Singer to Perform in Europe"? Explain why.

   _____

Name_____ Date_____

A. Read the newspaper article below. Underline the sentences that tell facts.

> DENVER, CO, Apr. 2—The National Park Service has announced plans to hire 20 new park rangers for Yellowstone National Park. The new rangers begin work on May 15. The rangers will be an important addition to the staff at the park, which is the oldest national park in the United States. It is estimated that over one million people will visit Yellowstone this summer.
>
> The new rangers' responsibilities will include presenting special programs about safety around bears. The rangers also plan to show slides of wildlife, geysers, and hot springs. The new rangers will maintain Yellowstone's 1,000 miles of trails. They will also direct many park activities. Horseback riding and fishing are the most popular activities among visitors.

B. Do you think it is important for the United States to have national parks? Write your opinion below. Support it with at least three reasons.

_____

_____

_____

_____

_____

_____

_____

_____

C. Find out two more facts about Yellowstone National Park. Write them below.

1. _____

_____

2. _____

_____

20 ▶ Using and Subscribing to Magazines

Skills 20.4–20.5

Exercise 80

Critical Thinking

A. Think about the kind of magazine you would create if you were the publisher. Then answer the questions below.

1. What would be the title of your magazine? _____

_____

2. What kinds of articles and information would you include in your magazine?

_____

3. Would you write any of the articles for your magazine? Explain. _____

_____

4. What are two examples of headlines that would be seen in your magazine?

_____

5. What kind of people would read your magazine? _____

_____

B. Create a subscription card for your magazine. Organize it any way you like. Include how much a subscription costs, the time periods for which a person can subscribe, and how to pay for the magazine. Write your subscription card below.

21 ▶ Figuring Out Word Meanings   Exercise 81

Skill 21.1   *Practice*

A. Read each sentence below. Then make an educated guess as to what the underlined word means, and circle the correct letter. Answer the questions.

1. "The restaurant offers a wide selection of salads, soups, and other <u>appetizers</u> for you to enjoy while you wait to be seated."
   The word <u>appetizers</u> means

   a. large sandwiches   **b.** steaks   **c.** small dishes enjoyed
                                                                before dinner

2. What is one clue that helped you make your decision?

   _____

3. "Guidebooks, maps, and <u>brochures</u> are located on the table next to the front desk."
   The word <u>brochures</u> means

   a. information booklets   **b.** snack foods   **c.** lists of foods served

4. What is one clue that helped you make your decision?

   _____

5. "We are not responsible for lost or stolen <u>articles</u>."
   The word <u>articles</u> means

   a. stories in a magazine   **b.** personal items   **c.** puzzle clues

6. What is one clue that helped you make your decision?

   _____

7. "Check your <u>itinerary</u> to make sure that you leave on the right bus."
   The word <u>itinerary</u> means

   a. luggage   **b.** schedule   **c.** local TV station

8. What is one clue that helped you make your decision?

   _____

B. Think of some words you have seen on menus or while traveling that you did not know. How did you figure out what these words meant? Write your answers on a separate sheet of paper.

21 ▶ Identifying Facts and Opinions

Skills 21.2–21.3

Exercise 82

Practice

A. Read each of the following statements. If it is a fact, write *fact* on the line. If it is an opinion, write *opinion* on the line.

1. Spaghetti is usually served with a sauce of some kind. _____

2. Tomato sauce with meatballs is the worst sauce for spaghetti. _____

3. Italian food is the best food in the world. _____

4. Mozzarella is a type of cheese often used in Italian cooking. _____

5. Spaghetti, linguini, fettuccine, and lasagne are examples of types of

   pasta. _____

6. The best kind of pasta is linguini. _____

7. Ari cooked linguini with marinara sauce tonight. _____

8. Ari's sauce turned out great. _____

B. Choose any one of the sentences in Part A. Write a paragraph on that topic, either giving more information or telling a story.

_____

_____

_____

_____

_____

_____

_____

_____

_____

_____

_____

_____

Name _____ Date _____

 21 ▶ Classifying Lists

Skill 21.4

Exercise 83

Critical Thinking

A. Four people are planning their vacations. Each one has written a list of things to pack. Read the lists. From the items listed, determine which city each person will visit. Choose from the cities listed in the box. Write the name of the city on the line.

Washington, D.C.	Honolulu, Hawaii
New York, New York	Paris, France

Bob's List
sunglasses
sunscreen lotion
bathing suit
beach towel

City: _____

Jessica's List
passport
French/English dictionary
umbrella
walking shoes

City: _____

Meryl's List
camera
film
sneakers
guide to U.S. Presidents and the White House

City: _____

Ricardo's List
camera
film
umbrella
Statue of Liberty guidebook

City: _____

B. Plan your own vacation. Think about where you would like to visit. Write a list of things to pack.

_____

_____

_____

_____

_____

_____

21 ▶ Writing a Letter

Skill 21.4

Exercise 84

Critical Thinking

Read this ad for a vacation hotel. Use the information to decide what it would be like to spend some time there. Then write a letter to a friend from this place. Tell your friend what you have been doing, what you plan to do, what kinds of meals you have had, and so on. (You may wish to use a dictionary to look up some words.)

> Special Winter Rates: $65 to $75 per person per night, based on double occupancy. Scenic bay views, complimentary continental breakfast and newspaper, heated pool, spa, sauna. Beaches, fishing, golf nearby. Valid January 1 through February 28, Sunday through Thursday nights only. Holidays excluded. Other restrictions may apply. Inn by the Sea, 9999 Coast Highway, Secret Beach, 800-555-5555.

22 ▶ Choosing the Reason

Skills 22.1–22.2

The sentences below came from personal messages. What do you think was the reason for each message? Choose from the reasons listed in the box. Write the reason on the line.

invitation	response to invitation	sympathy card
postcard from vacation	birthday card	thank-you note

1. Mr. and Mrs. A. A. Miller request the honor of your presence at the wedding of their daughter. _____

2. I was so sorry to hear about your loss. I, too, will miss Tweety. He was a wonderful parakeet. _____

3. The clock you sent will be among my most treasured possessions.

_____

4. This is the most interesting city we have visited so far. The art museums are amazing! _____

5. I am sorry to say that I cannot attend the celebration for your parents' fiftieth wedding anniversary. _____

6. We wish you the happiest birthday ever. _____

7. The flowers are charming. I have given them a place of honor in the family room. _____

8. I had no idea Paris could be so romantic! _____

9. We will be delighted to attend the party for your son's graduation from high school. _____

10. The memory of your beloved father will always remind us that a sense of humor is the key to enjoying life. _____

22 ▶ Brainstorming Phrases

Skills 22.1–22.2

Complete the three idea webs below with words or phrases that would be useful in your personal messages. Some examples are already given.

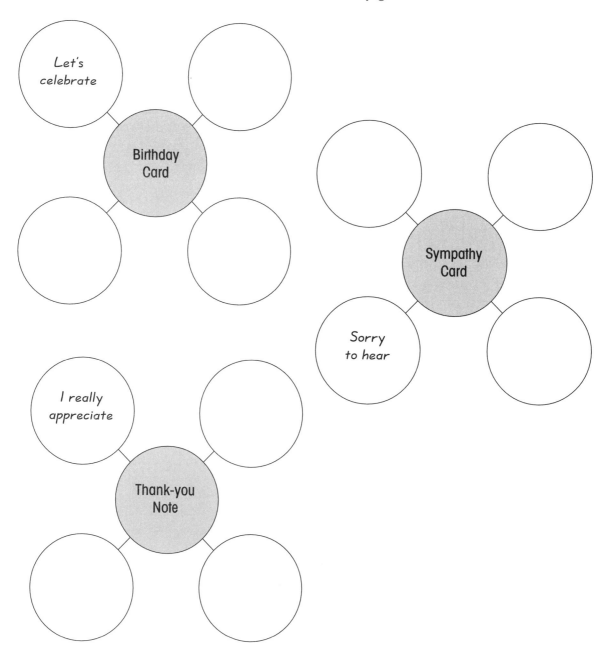

22 ▶ Writing Social Notes

Skills 22.1–22.2

Exercise 87

Critical Thinking

A. Write an invitation to an event. It might be a birthday, a Fourth of July party, a Saturday barbecue, or a slumber party. Do not forget to include answers to *who, what, why, where, when,* and *how.*

_____

_____

_____

_____

_____

_____

_____

_____

_____

B. Now write a response to the invitation. You may either accept or decline. If you accept, be sure to let the other person know you are looking forward to the event. If you decline, be sure to let the other person know how sorry you are that you cannot make it.

_____

_____

_____

_____

_____

_____

_____

_____

_____

22 ▶ Writing Personal Messages

Skills 22.3–22.6

Exercise 88

Critical Thinking

A. You have a friend who runs in marathons. While competing in his latest marathon, he injured himself and could not continue. He had spent many weeks preparing for the race and was very disappointed. What message would you write to him?

_____

_____

_____

_____

B. You are spending some time at a friend's vacation house. The town where you are staying is having a festival at the same time you are there. What kind of postcard message would you send to your family back home?

_____

_____

_____

_____

C. You took a job that required you to move to a city across the country. It has been hard leaving your friends and family behind. However, you like where you live, and your new job is great. Write a short letter to a friend about your experience.

_____

_____

_____

_____

Name_____ Date_____

 23 ▶ **Writing About Strengths and Weaknesses**   **Exercise 89**

Skill 23.1   *Critical Thinking*

A. Think about your own strengths and weaknesses. Make a list under each heading below.

          What I Like About Myself   **What I Don't Like About Myself**

_____   _____

_____   _____

_____   _____

_____   _____

_____   _____

_____   _____

_____   _____

_____   _____

B. Now think about the items in the second list. Is there any way you can change? Write a paragraph telling how you can improve those things you do not like about yourself.

_____

_____

_____

_____

_____

_____

_____

23 ▶ Writing Positive Criticisms   Exercise 90

Skill 23.1   *Practice*

Each of the following criticisms is negative. Rewrite it, making it sound kinder and more positive. The first one is done for you.

1. Brad's house looks as if he never gets around to dusting.

   *Dusting is not important in Brad's life.*_____

2. That shirt makes Ian look like an elephant.

   _____

3. Ellie's office looks as if a cyclone hit it.

   _____

4. Dennis plays the worst music I have ever heard.

   _____

5. The decorations in that restaurant are really tacky.

   _____

6. Lizelle wears far too much makeup.

   _____

7. Laura cooks the worst meals I have ever tasted.

   _____

8. Gina is very clumsy on the dance floor.

   _____

9. Noah talks too much.

   _____

10. Matthew is the worst actor in our drama class.

   _____

Name _____   Date _____

 23 **Role Playing a Personal Critique**   **Exercise 91**
Skill 23.2   *Critical Thinking*

A friend of yours has asked for an honest answer to the question, "What's wrong with me?" What would you say? How would your friend respond? Write the dialogue. Then act it out for the class.

Your friend: *What's wrong with me?* _____

You: _____

_____

_____

Your friend: _____

_____

_____

You: _____

_____

_____

Your friend: _____

_____

_____

You: _____

_____

_____

Your friend: _____

_____

_____

You: _____

_____

_____

23 ▶ Making Recommendations

Skill 23.2

Exercise 92

Practice

Read each paragraph below. Then answer the questions.

1. Four people are in a car, two in front and two in back. During a conversation, the driver keeps turning around to make eye contact with the people in the back. Kent, one of the passengers, is getting very nervous because he thinks a driver should watch the road. What, if anything, should Kent say? Why?

    _____

    _____

2. A restaurant gives each customer a card asking about the service. Debi's server was fast, but he forgot to bring the salad dressing on the side, as she had asked. She already spoke to the server about it, and he apologized. What should Debi write on the card? Why?

    _____

    _____

3. Spiro's best friend, Ben, has the habit of pushing his food onto his fork with his fingers. It doesn't really bother Spiro, but now Ben has been invited to a dinner. It is important to Ben because he will be meeting his girlfriend's family for the first time. What, if anything, should Spiro say? Why?

    _____

    _____

4. Georgia's friend Bette cracks her knuckles about three times an hour. Georgia suspects the knuckle-cracking is one reason for Bette's being unable to keep a job. What, if anything, should Georgia say? Why?

    _____

    _____

5. Colin has an office next to Caroline's office. Caroline wears a lovely perfume every day, but Colin is allergic to it. What, if anything, should Colin say? Why?

    _____

    _____